DIGITAL MARKETING FOR DENTISTS: A COMPREHENSIVE GUIDE

DIBAKAR BALA

Made with ♥ on the Notion Press Platform
www.notionpress.com

Contents

CHAPTER ONE

Introduction to Digital Marketing for Dentists

Digital marketing is the use of digital technologies and channels to promote products or services. In the world of dentistry, digital marketing can be a powerful tool for attracting new patients and growing your dental practice. With the right strategies and tactics, you can reach potential patients where they are online, build trust and credibility for your practice, and drive more traffic and conversions to your dental website.

In this chapter, we will explore the basics of digital marketing and how it can benefit dentists. We will also discuss the key principles to consider as you develop your digital marketing plan, and provide an overview of the chapters that follow.

Digital marketing offers a wide range of opportunities for dentists to reach potential patients. Through content marketing, you can educate and inform potential patients about oral health and the services your practice offers. Social media platforms like Facebook, Twitter, and Instagram can be used to connect with potential patients and build your brand. And by optimizing your website for search engines, you can increase your online visibility and make it easier for potential patients to find you.

In addition to these tactics, email marketing and paid advertising can also be effective ways to reach potential patients and drive traffic and conversions to your website. By collecting email addresses and creating targeted ads, you can stay in touch with potential and current patients and keep your practice top-of-mind.

Overall, digital marketing offers a wealth of opportunities for dentists to reach new patients and grow their practice. In the chapters that follow, we will explore these strategies and tactics in more detail and provide guidance on how to implement them effectively.

CHAPTER TWO

Developing a Strong Foundation with a Well-Designed Website

Your dental website is often the first impression potential patients have of your practice, so it's important to make it a good one. A well-designed website can help to build trust and credibility for your practice, and make it easy for potential patients to find the information they need.

In this chapter, we will discuss the key elements of a well-designed dental website and provide tips for creating a user-friendly, professional-looking site.

One of the most important elements of a dental website is its design. A clean, modern design can help to create a professional and trustworthy image for your practice. Make sure to use high-quality images and graphics, and avoid using too many colors or fonts, which can make the site look cluttered and unprofessional.

In addition to its design, a dental website should be easy to navigate. Potential patients should be able to find the information they need quickly and easily. This means organizing your content into clear, intuitive sections and using clear, descriptive headings and subheadings.

Another key element of a well-designed dental website is mobile-friendliness. With more and more people accessing the internet from their smartphones and tablets, it's important to make sure your website is optimized for mobile devices. This means ensuring that the site loads quickly, and that the content is easy to read and navigate on smaller screens.

Finally, it's important to include clear calls-to-action (CTAs) on your dental website. CTAs are buttons or links that encourage visitors to take a specific action, such as booking an appointment or subscribing to your email list. Make sure to place your CTAs prominently on the site, and use clear, compelling language to encourage visitors to click.

Overall, a well-designed dental website is an essential foundation for your digital marketing efforts. By creating a professional, user-friendly, and mobile-friendly site, you can build trust and credibility for your practice and make it easier for potential patients to find the information they need.

CHAPTER THREE

Creating a Content Marketing Strategy

Content marketing is a type of digital marketing that involves creating and sharing valuable, informative, and engaging content with the goal of attracting and retaining a clearly-defined audience. In the world of dentistry, content marketing can be a powerful way to educate potential patients about oral health and the services your practice offers.

In this chapter, we will discuss the principles of content marketing for dentists and provide tips for creating and sharing effective content.

The first step in creating a content marketing strategy for your dental practice is to identify your target audience. Who are the potential patients you want to reach? What are their needs, interests, and pain points when it comes to oral health and dental care? By understanding your target audience, you can create content that resonates with them and addresses their specific concerns.

Next, it's important to identify the goals of your content marketing efforts. Are you looking to attract new patients, build trust and credibility for your practice, or drive traffic and conversions to your website? By setting clear goals, you can create content that aligns with your objectives and helps you achieve your desired outcomes.

Once you have identified your target audience and goals, you can begin creating content. For dentists, this could include blog posts, videos, infographics, or other types of content that provide valuable information and advice about oral health and dental care. When creating content, it's important to focus on providing value to your audience and addressing their specific needs and interests. Avoid using overly promotional language or making exaggerated claims, which can erode trust and credibility.

Once you have created your content, it's important to share it with your target audience. This could involve posting it on your website, sharing it on social media, or emailing it to your email list. By promoting your content and making it easy for potential patients to find, you can increase its reach and impact.

Overall, content marketing can be a powerful tool for dentists. By creating and sharing valuable, informative content, you can educate potential patients and build trust and credibility for your practice. With the right content marketing strategy, you can attract more qualified leads and drive more traffic and conversions to your website.

CHAPTER FOUR

Search Engine Optimization for Dentists

Search engine optimization (SEO) is the practice of optimizing your website and its content to rank higher in search engine results pages (SERPs). By making your website more visible and relevant to search engines like Google, you can increase the chances that potential patients will find you when they're searching for a dentist online.

In this chapter, we will discuss the principles of SEO for dentists and provide tips for improving your website's visibility and ranking in search results.

One of the key principles of SEO is to create high-quality, relevant content. Search engines like Google use complex algorithms to determine the relevance and quality of a website's content. By creating content that is informative, accurate, and well-written, you can improve your website's visibility and ranking in search results.

In addition to creating high-quality content, it's important to optimize your website's meta tags and keywords. Meta tags are short pieces of HTML code that provide information about your website to search engines. By including relevant keywords in your meta tags, you can improve your website's visibility and ranking for those keywords.

Another key principle of SEO is to build backlinks. Backlinks are links from other websites that point to your website. Search engines use backlinks as a sign of a website's authority and relevance. By building backlinks from high-quality, relevant websites, you can improve your website's visibility and ranking in search results.

Finally, it's important to monitor and analyze the results of your SEO efforts. By using tools like Google Analytics, you can track your website's traffic, ranking, and other key metrics. By analyzing this data, you can identify areas for improvement and make adjustments to your SEO strategy to drive better results.

Overall, SEO is an important aspect of digital marketing for dentists. By optimizing your website and its content for search engines, you can increase your online visibility and make it easier for potential patients to find you. By following the principles and tips outlined in this chapter, you can improve your website's ranking and drive more qualified traffic to your site.

CHAPTER FIVE

Using Social Media to Engage with Potential Patients

Social media platforms like Facebook, Twitter, and Instagram are a great way for dentists to connect with potential patients and build your brand. By sharing interesting and relevant content, engaging with followers, and responding to comments and messages, you can create a positive online presence for your dental practice.

In this chapter, we will discuss the principles of using social media for dentists and provide tips for creating and implementing a successful social media strategy.

One of the key principles of using social media for dentists is to identify the platforms that are most relevant to your target audience. Different social media platforms have different audiences, so it's important to choose the ones that are most likely to reach the potential patients you want to attract.

Once you have identified the social media platforms that are right for your practice, it's important to create a content strategy. This means deciding what type of content you will share, how often you will post, and what tone and voice you will use. It's a good idea to create a mix of content that is informative, entertaining, and engaging, and to post regularly to keep your social media accounts active and engaging.

In addition to creating and sharing content, it's important to engage with your followers on social media. This means responding to comments and messages, sharing user-generated content, and asking questions to encourage interaction and engagement. By building a community of followers on social media, you can create a positive online presence for your practice and establish yourself as a trusted resource for oral health information.

Finally, it's important to monitor and analyze the results of your social media efforts. By using tools like Facebook Insights or Twitter Analytics, you can track the engagement, reach, and other key metrics of your social media posts. By analyzing this data, you can identify which types of content are most effective and make adjustments to your strategy to improve your results.

Overall, social media can be a powerful tool for dentists. By creating and sharing interesting and relevant content, and engaging with followers, you can build a positive online presence for your practice and establish yourself as a trusted resource for oral health information. By following the principles and tips outlined in this chapter, you can create a successful social media strategy for your dental practice.

CHAPTER SIX

Email Marketing for Dental Practices

Email marketing is a powerful way for dentists to stay in touch with potential and current patients. By collecting email addresses from your website, social media, or in-office sign-up sheets, you can send newsletters, appointment reminders, and special offers to keep your practice top-of-mind for patients.

In this chapter, we will discuss the principles of email marketing for dentists and provide tips for creating and implementing an effective email marketing campaign.

One of the key principles of email marketing for dentists is to collect email addresses from potential and current patients. This can be done through sign-up forms on your website, social media, or in-office. It's important to make it clear to patients why you are collecting their email address, and to provide them with an easy way to opt out if they do not want to receive emails from your practice.

Once you have collected a list of email addresses, it's important to segment your list into different groups. This means dividing your email list into smaller sub-lists based on factors like demographics, interests, and behavior. By segmenting your email list, you can create more targeted and effective campaigns that are more likely to resonate with specific groups of patients.

Next, it's important to create a content strategy for your email marketing campaigns. This means deciding what type of content you will send to your email list, how often you will send it, and what tone and voice you will use. It's a good idea to create a mix of content that is informative, engaging, and actionable, and to send emails regularly to keep your practice top-of-mind for patients.

In addition to creating and sending emails, it's important to monitor and analyze the results of your campaigns. By using tools like Google Analytics, you can track the open rate, click-through rate, and other key metrics of your emails. By analyzing this data, you can identify which types of content are most effective and make adjustments to your strategy to improve your results.

Overall, email marketing can be a powerful tool for dentists. By collecting email addresses and sending regular, targeted emails, you can stay in touch with potential and current patients and keep your practice top-of-mind. By following the principles and tips outlined in this chapter, you can create an effective email marketing campaign for your dental practice.

CHAPTER SEVEN

Paid Advertising for Dentists

Paid advertising, such as Google AdWords or Facebook Ads, can be a great way for dentists to quickly reach a targeted audience of potential patients. By creating relevant and compelling ads and targeting them to specific demographics and locations, you can drive more traffic and conversions to your website.

In this chapter, we will discuss the principles of paid advertising for dentists and provide tips for creating and implementing successful ad campaigns.

One of the key principles of paid advertising is to set clear goals and objectives. Before you start creating ads, it's important to decide what you want to achieve with your campaigns. Are you looking to drive traffic to your website, generate leads, or promote a specific service or offer? By setting clear goals, you can create ads that align with your objectives and help you achieve your desired outcomes.

Next, it's important to identify the platforms and formats that are most relevant to your target audience and goals. Different advertising platforms and formats have different strengths and weaknesses, so it's important to choose the ones that are most likely to reach and engage your target audience.

Once you have identified the platforms and formats that are right for your campaigns, it's important to create compelling ads. This means using clear, compelling language, high-quality images, and strong calls-to-action (CTAs) to encourage potential patients to take the desired action. It's also important to use relevant keywords and target your ads to specific demographics and locations to ensure that they are shown to the right people.

In addition to creating ads, it's important to monitor and analyze the results of your campaigns. By using tools like Google Analytics or Facebook Ads Manager, you can track the performance of your ads in terms of impressions, clicks, conversions, and other key metrics. By analyzing this data, you can identify which ads are performing well and make adjustments to your campaigns to improve your results.

Overall, paid advertising can be a powerful tool for dentists. By creating relevant and compelling ads and targeting them to the right audience, you can quickly drive traffic and conversions to your website. By following the principles and tips outlined in this chapter, you can create successful ad campaigns for your dental practice.

CHAPTER EIGHT

Measuring and Analyzing the Results

One of the key principles of digital marketing is to measure and analyze the results of your efforts. By tracking key metrics and analyzing data, you can identify which strategies and tactics are working well, and which ones need improvement. This information can help you make informed decisions about how to allocate your marketing budget and resources, and how to adjust your strategies to drive better results.

In this chapter, we will discuss the key metrics and tools that can be used to measure and analyze the results of your digital marketing efforts.

One of the key metrics to track for your digital marketing efforts is website traffic. This refers to the number of visitors who come to your website from various sources, such as search engines, social media, or paid advertising. By tracking website traffic, you can see how many people are visiting your site and where they are coming from.

Another important metric to track is engagement. This refers to the level of interaction and engagement that your website and social media content receives. For example, you can track the number of likes, comments, and shares on your social media posts, or the number of clicks and conversions on your website. By tracking engagement, you can see how well your content is resonating with your target audience.

In addition to traffic and engagement, it's important to track conversions. This refers to the number of website visitors who take a specific action, such as filling out a contact form or making a purchase. By tracking conversions, you can see how effective your digital marketing efforts are at driving desired actions from potential patients.

To track these metrics, you can use tools like Google Analytics, Facebook Insights, or Twitter Analytics. These tools provide detailed data and insights about your website and social media performance, and can help you identify areas for improvement and make data-driven decisions about your digital marketing strategies.

Overall, measuring and analyzing the results of your digital marketing efforts is essential for improving your performance and driving better results. By tracking key metrics and using data-driven tools, you can make informed decisions about how to allocate your marketing budget and resources

CHAPTER NINE

Advanced tactics for driving traffic and conversions

In this chapter, we will explore some advanced tactics for driving traffic and increasing conversions on your dental website. These tactics are designed to help you take your digital marketing efforts to the next level and continue to grow your dental practice.

One tactic that can be effective for driving traffic to your website is to create a network of dental bloggers who are willing to share your content and promote your practice on their own blogs and social media channels. This can help you reach a wider audience and increase the visibility of your website.

Another tactic that can be effective is to use social media to engage with potential patients. This can include responding to comments and questions on your own social media pages, as well as engaging with other dental professionals and potential patients on relevant industry forums and discussion boards.

Another tactic that can help drive traffic and conversions is to use paid advertising. This can include running ads on social media platforms, search engines, and other websites that are relevant to your target audience. By carefully targeting your ads, you can ensure that they are seen by the right people and increase the likelihood of conversions.

Finally, it is important to regularly measure and analyze the results of your digital marketing efforts. This can help you identify what is working well and what needs to be improved, and make adjustments to your strategy accordingly. By using tools like Google Analytics, you can track key metrics such as website traffic, conversion rates, and the sources of your traffic, and use this information to continually improve your digital marketing efforts.

In conclusion, these advanced tactics can help you drive traffic and increase conversions on your dental website, and continue to grow your dental practice. By implementing these tactics and regularly measuring and analyzing the results, you can ensure that your digital marketing efforts are effective and continue to evolve and improve over time.

CHAPTER TEN

How I Can Help Your Dental Practice Grow

In this chapter, we will discuss how I can help your dental practice grow with digital marketing. As a specialist in digital marketing for dentists, I have the knowledge, expertise, and experience to help your practice reach its full potential online.

I can help you develop a strong foundation with a well-designed website that is optimized for search engines and easy for potential patients to navigate. I can also help you create a comprehensive content marketing strategy that will attract and engage potential patients, and drive traffic and conversions to your website.

I am also experienced in using social media to engage with potential patients and build relationships with your target audience. I can help you create engaging and relevant content for your social media channels, and develop a social media strategy that will help you reach your goals.

In addition, I can help you with paid advertising on platforms such as Google Ads and social media, and ensure that your ads are targeted and effective. I can also help you measure and analyze the results of your digital marketing efforts, and make recommendations for how to improve and optimize your strategy.

If you are interested in working with me to help grow your dental practice with digital marketing, please don't hesitate to reach out. I would be happy to discuss your goals and needs, and provide a customized plan for achieving success online.

Concluding Thoughts And Next Steps

In this chapter, we will summarize the key points covered in this book and discuss next steps for continuing to grow your dental practice with digital marketing.

Throughout this book, we have discussed the importance of digital marketing for dentists, and how to develop a strong foundation with a well-designed website, create a content marketing strategy, optimize for search engines, and engage with potential patients on social media. We have also covered the use of paid advertising and the importance of measuring and analyzing the results of your digital marketing efforts.

In order to successfully grow your dental practice with digital marketing, it is important to regularly evaluate and update your strategy, and continue to learn and adapt to new trends and developments in the field. By staying up-to-date with the latest best practices and techniques, you can ensure that your digital marketing efforts are effective and continue to drive traffic and conversions to your website.

In conclusion, digital marketing is an essential tool for dentists looking to grow their practice and reach potential patients. By implementing the strategies and tactics discussed in this book, you can take your digital marketing efforts to the next level and continue to drive traffic and conversions to your website.

Printed by Libri Plureos GmbH in Hamburg,
Germany